CLASSROOM HOW-TO

PREPARING FOR AN EXAM

VALERIE BODDEN | ILLUSTRATIONS BY NATE WILLIAMS

CREATIVE ✿ EDUCATION

Published by Creative Education
P.O. Box 227, Mankato, Minnesota 56002
Creative Education is an imprint of The Creative Company
www.thecreativecompany.us

Design and production by Liddy Walseth
Art direction by Rita Marshall
Printed in the United States of America

Illustrations by Nate Williams © 2014

Library of Congress Cataloging-in-Publication Data
Bodden, Valerie.
Preparing for an exam / Valerie Bodden.
p. cm. – (Classroom how-to)
Includes bibliographical references and index.
Summary: An approachable guide to help master and apply the
writing, speaking, and listening skills involved in studying and
retaining the necessary information for any test or exam.
ISBN 978-1-60818-282-4
1. Test-taking skills—Juvenile literature. 2. Examinations—Study
guides—Juvenile literature. I. Title.
LB3060.57.B64 2014
371.26—dc23 2013029621

CCSS: RI.5.1, 2, 3, 7, 8, 9; RH.6-8.1, 6, 9; W.5.1, 2, 3, 4, 5, 7, 8, 9, 10;
W.6.1, 2, 4, 7, 8, 9; SL.6.1, 3, 4, 6

First Edition
2 4 6 8 9 7 5 3 1

TABLE OF CONTENTS

4

INTRODUCTION

7

TESTS: TOOLS OR TORTURE?

15

BE PREPARED

25

DOWN TO THE WIRE

35

TEST TIME

45

GLOSSARY

46

SELECTED BIBLIOGRAPHY

47

READ MORE & WEBSITES

48

INDEX

HOMEWORK. *Tests.* Speeches. **Papers.**

Does it sometimes feel like you face an endless list of tasks to complete for

school? And why? To make your teachers happy? Well, yes, completing your

work is likely to make your teachers happy. But that is not the only reason

teachers assign work. Believe it or not, writing papers, taking tests, and mak-

ing speeches benefits you, too. Every time you complete one of these tasks,

you learn something more about how to do it, and you become more pre-

pared to do it again in the future—in high school, college, and even possibly

your career. But more than that, these tasks teach you how to learn, how to

study, how to find information, and how to present your viewpoint. And such

skills will help you not only in the classroom but also in life.

Exams, for instance, help to ensure that you've learned the material being taught in a specific class. And studying for an exam also helps you find ways to retain information. And that's a skill that will help in nearly every aspect of your life—from remembering how to execute a play in basketball to learning your lines for the school theater production. But how do you know what you will be tested on? When should you start studying for an exam? And how do you go about learning the material you need to know? Learning the answers to these questions will help you turn in an exam that will make your teacher happy— and teach you something in the process!

TESTS: TOOLS OR TORTURE?

Unless your school is highly unusual, you have probably already taken a number of tests during the course of your educational career. But now that you're older, you might be finding that tests are getting harder and require more studying. That's because the material you are covering is more advanced—and also because your teachers are ready to challenge you more.

But why? Why do teachers insist on giving tests? Couldn't they just teach a lesson and then move on? Quite simply, tests help your teacher determine whether you've learned what she's been teaching. They make you **accountable** for mastering the material. And ultimately, your tests—combined with your other work, of course—help your teacher decide if you are ready to move on to the next grade level and, eventually, to graduate. But you're not the only one being evaluated here. A test can also help a teacher determine whether she has taught the material effectively—or if she needs to go back and review certain concepts or try a different teaching method. Tests can even be used to evaluate the performance of an entire school system.

Once you've graduated from high school, you probably won't be done taking tests. Many colleges require students to take entrance exams. Or you might need to complete **standardized tests** such as the American College Test (ACT) or Scholastic Achievement Test (SAT) before being admitted to a university. The good news is, your scores on such tests can actually earn you the right to take certain classes, enter prestigious programs, or win scholarship money. And even if you don't think you'll go to college, you may have to take a **civil service exam** to obtain a government job. In the private sector, an employer may require you to take a test to prove you've mastered a specific skill or that you deserve a promotion—and a raise! So it pays to learn how to take tests now.

Generally speaking, the more tests you take, the better you'll get at taking them. In addition, taking a test requires you to study—and studying helps you remember what you've learned. Believe it or not, the information you learn now will be useful in the future. Studying verb tenses may not seem exciting now, but it will sure come in handy when you apply for journalism school. Learning Newton's laws of motion may sound like a snooze, but someday you'll make use of that information in your college physics lab. Algebra may appear pointless, but you'll need a strong math foundation for a career in engineering. At the same time, taking tests can actually help you discover which

"IF A MAN EMPTIES HIS PURSE INTO HIS HEAD, NO MAN CAN TAKE IT AWAY FROM HIM. AN INVESTMENT IN KNOWLEDGE ALWAYS PAYS THE BEST INTEREST."

— Benjamin Franklin

STUDY THOSE AREAS

subjects you enjoy and are good at. As you get further into your academic career, you will have opportunities to study those areas in greater depth.

Despite the benefits that can be reaped from taking exams, most people still do not like them. And many people are downright terrified of them. A little test anxiety isn't necessarily a bad thing—it can get your **adrenaline** pumping and help you stay alert and focused throughout the exam. But excessive anxiety is unhealthy. It can cause students to develop a fear of being seen as stupid, to worry about disappointing their parents, or to believe that they'll be a failure in life. Such anxiety can cause physical symptoms such as a racing heartbeat, sweaty palms, and upset stomach. It can also interfere with test performance, sometimes causing students to "blank out" and forget everything when it comes time to take the test. If you have been in this situation, take heart: your case is not hopeless. There are techniques you can use to help alleviate your anxiety. In the long run, thorough preparation for a test is the best cure for test anxiety—so read on.

Sometimes, though, it may seem that there just isn't enough time to study. You have other homework to complete, papers to write, sports practices to attend, friends to hang out with. It might seem that it's just too hard to fit studying in until the night before the test. And unfortunately, by then it's usually too late. Cramming is the worst way to study for a test. You may think that you can learn a lot by glancing through your books and notes the night before a test, but the truth is that you probably can't. According to some experts, you'll remember only 20 percent of what you study when you cram—and 20 percent doesn't make for a very good grade. And even if you do manage to remember enough information to get a good grade on the exam, you will forget nearly all of it by the time you have handed in the test. No big

TERRIFIC TEST-TAKING!

deal? It is if you have a final exam that covers the same material or if the course is cumulative—meaning that one concept builds on the last—like math. In addition, if you suffer from test anxiety, cramming is likely to make it worse, as you will enter the test feeling unprepared and nervous—not to mention tired from staying up late.

But perhaps you've studied well in advance of a test and know your material cold—and still do poorly on an exam. In this case, it may not be your mastery of the subject matter that is at fault but rather your test-taking skills. You see, in order to do well on a test, you need to know not only *what* is on the test but also *how* to take a test. Perhaps you are spending too much time on questions that count for only a small part of your overall score. Maybe you aren't reading directions carefully. Or perhaps essay questions just stump you. Don't worry, test-taking skills—like study habits—can be learned. And once they are, you'll be surprised at how terrific (or at least not as terrifying) test-taking is!

CHAPTER
TWO

BE PREPARED

When it comes to studying, the sooner you get started, the better. In fact, you should start studying your course materials (notes, books, handouts, lab reports) beginning the first day of class, even if your first test is days, weeks, or months away. Why? The more often you see and study something, the better you will remember it. Think about the people you know, for example. You'll probably never forget your best friend's name—you use it every day. But the next time you're at the store, look at the cashier's nametag. Then try to remember his name a few days later. If you haven't used it, you will most likely draw a blank. Frequently reviewing information helps commit it to your long-term memory—which is where you want it during a test. Frequent studying also helps you identify areas where you have trouble so that you can ask for help now and so that you know where you'll need to concentrate your effort when test time comes around. Plus, the more you study now, the less you'll have to study right before a test—and the more confident you'll be that you know the material inside and out.

One of the best ways to ensure that you'll regularly review your material (and not just say you will) is to set up a study plan. First, get yourself a calendar and mark the test dates on it (if your teachers give you that information in advance). That way, you'll know when you need to set aside time to do your most intense studying. You'll also discover dates when you might have tests in two different subjects—so you won't be surprised and have to skip studying for one in order to prepare for the other.

Then plan a time each day for studying. You don't have to study every subject every time you sit down to study, but it's helpful to review each subject at least once a week. Don't plan on marathon study sessions, though. After 45 minutes or so, you'll probably feel your brain begin to fizzle, and you'll no longer be able to concentrate on the task at hand. Instead, be sure to take short breaks or to schedule several short study periods throughout the day rather than one long one. Although the time of day you choose to study may depend in large part on when you are not busy doing something else, try to schedule your study time for when you are at your best. If you're a morning person, spend some time studying before school in the morning. If you're a night owl, make your study time in the evening (though maybe not right before bed, or

you might find yourself dozing halfway through your biology notes).

As you set up your study schedule, also consider your study conditions. You are probably not going to be able to give your full concentration to your social studies book if you are working

at the kitchen table while your parents are preparing supper, your older brother is doing a drum solo on the counter, and your baby sister is grabbing at your book. Instead, you need to find a quiet, comfortable (but not too comfortable— you don't want to fall asleep) spot to hit the books. Maybe your bedroom is your quiet haven. Or maybe your parents have an office they will let you use. Sometimes you might need to get out of the house altogether and use a study room at the library.

If the idea of studying well in

advance of an exam (and sometimes before you even know when the exam will *be*) is new to you, then you're probably wondering what exactly you should study. One of the best ways to ensure that you remember new material is to review your class notes and your textbook. If you haven't been taking notes in class, start. Taking notes ensures that you will pay attention to the instructor. And writing down what he says helps you to remember the information longer. After class, you might even choose to rewrite and organize your notes. Not only will this make studying easier later, but it will also give you another chance to work with—and remember—the information.

As you study your notes, pay special attention to material your teacher covered at length or repeated several times—this is likely important information (in other words, likely to appear on a test). Your textbook has similar ways of indicating important information—watch especially for headings and bolded words. You might take notes from your textbook as well so that at test time you'll have everything in one notebook. Taking notes on the text also helps you focus on what you are reading rather than simply looking at the words without taking in their meaning. In addition to taking and reviewing notes, be sure to complete your daily homework assignments. Teachers give these assignments for a reason—and it's not to keep you from having fun. Often, similar (or even the same) questions

or problems will appear on a test. So doing the work now will give you an advantage later.

As you review, keep in mind that different people learn best in different ways. Some people are visual learn-ers—they need to see something in order to learn it well. Such learners can often "picture" their notes or textbook pages in their heads. **Audi-tory** learners, on the other hand, learn material best when they hear it. They may even "hear" their teacher's voice in their head when they try to recall information. While visual and auditory learners each rely heavily on a single sense, **kinesthetic** learners use their whole body. They learn best by actually working with the information they have been given.

Of course, you probably use a combination of learning styles. But you might also recognize that one dominates. Maybe you have to reread instructions several times in order to understand them, but you need to hear the same instructions only once to follow them. Don't be afraid to take advantage of your dominant learning style by studying in a way that appeals to it. Visual learners, for example, can benefit from rereading and color-coding notes, drawing pictures or diagrams, watching videos, or study-ing charts and illustrations. Listening to a teacher's lecture, discussing new information with a friend, reading out loud, or making an audio recording of notes are methods that can help auditory learners. And rewriting notes, physically touching objects (a model planet, for example), working out while studying, or **role-playing** can get a kin-esthetic learner involved in her studies.

Depending on your learning style, you might find joining (or forming) a study group beneficial. Auditory learners, especially, can benefit from the opportunity to talk through the in-formation they've been given in class. Study groups give you a chance to compare notes with other students in your class, to ask questions about con-

PEOPLE LEARN BEST IN DIFFERENT WAYS

cepts that confuse you, and even to practice testing one another on the material. Taking part in a study group can also help you stay **motivated** and accountable for studying on a more regular basis.

When forming a study group, make sure that everyone in the group is equally motivated to study. While it can be fun to study with friends, beware of the danger that your study time will turn into a gab session—or a video game marathon. Make sure that everyone in the group will be able to stay on topic for the agreed upon length of time—then celebrate afterward with social time.

To keep your study group sessions running smoothly, follow these tips:

1. Find a quiet place to meet. But make sure that your group will be allowed to talk. The stands at a football game are too loud. And the library reading room is too quiet. But you might use a study room at the library or meet at a group member's (quiet) house. A teacher might even let you use his empty classroom during lunch.

2. Limit your group's size to four to six members. More than that and it might be difficult to give everyone a chance to participate.

3. Have a plan for each meeting.

Will you review the week's notes? Work on practice problems? Talk about a reading assignment? Having a plan in place ensures that everyone will show up prepared.

No matter how you study, be sure to pay attention to areas that give you trouble—and seek help for them. Sitting around and fretting that you'll do poorly on the test because you don't understand something won't do you any good. So speak up. Ask your teacher to clarify a point during class, to help you work a problem after school, or to suggest further reading to help you better understand a specific topic. Putting the extra time into mastering difficult areas now will keep you from panicking when you learn that you'll need to know them for the test. And that's the whole point of advanced preparation—being prepared now so that you don't have to panic later!

"EDUCATION IS NOT SOMETHING THAT IS DONE FOR A STUDENT OR TO A STUDENT. IT IS WHAT THE STUDENT DOES FOR HIMSELF IN DEVELOPING HIS OWN POWERS. TEACHERS CAN HELP; SO CAN A CURRICULUM AND AN ATMOSPHERE OF DEVOTION TO THINGS OF THE MIND. BUT ULTIMATELY THE PROBLEM IS UTTERLY THE STUDENT'S."

— Charles W. Colson

DOWN TO THE WIRE

So you've spent time each week reviewing your notes and textbook. Now, test day approaches. What do you do? Depending on how big the test is (and how much of your final grade it will determine), you need to start your intense studying anywhere from a few days (for a small quiz) to two weeks (for a final exam) before the test.

But what exactly should you study now that test day is looming? After all, you may have covered three or four chapters of a textbook or several weeks of class notes since your last test—and that's a lot of information to try to remember. So, you need to figure out which areas are most important—and therefore likely to appear on the test. The best way to do this is to simply ask your teacher. After all, she made the test, and she may be willing to give you a detailed summary of what topics it will cover. Maybe she'll even hand out a study guide or make available exams from the previous year for you to review. If so, pay attention to the types of information students were tested on—did they need to know dates, names, or minor details? You'll probably need to know much the same thing this year.

Even if your teacher remains silent

on what to expect on the test, never fear. There are still ways to figure out what you should know. If you've already taken a test for this class (or if you've had this teacher for a previous class), you probably have at least some idea of the types of questions she asks. Review some of your old tests to get an idea of what kinds of information she generally looks for. For example, if your last three math tests had lots of story problems on them, you can expect that this one probably will, too. Even if you haven't had this teacher or taken a test for this class before, other students have. Find one of them and ask them about the kinds of tests your teacher gives. Someone might even have an old test available for you to look at (but make sure this is not against your school's policy first).

Paying close attention in class can also give you a good idea of what to expect on a test. If your teacher goes over the same material several times, there's a good bet you'll see a few questions dedicated to that material on the test. She might even give you a clue to the material's importance, such as, "Make sure to remember this." If she does, you should take her advice. Anything your teacher writes on the board is likely to appear on a test, too, so write it down. Your homework assignments can tip you off as well, as can major headings and vocabulary words in your textbook.

Once you have figured out the topics that are likely to appear on the test, concentrate your studies on those areas. Keep yourself organized and on the right subjects by making a study outline. The outline should list

the major concepts you need to focus on for the test. For each major topic, also include relevant details, facts, dates, names, formulas, and definitions that you may need to know. The study outline allows you to keep all your important information in one place so that as you study you won't be distracted—or overwhelmed—by all the other material. Moreover, the simple act of compiling the outline gives you one more chance to see and work with the information—which means one more chance to remember it.

In addition to studying what's going to be on the test, it can be helpful to know the test's format ahead of time. Will it be multiple-choice, true and false, matching, or essay questions? Here again, your teacher is the best source of information. But if she

won't give you a hint at the types of questions to expect, you might look over your old tests from the class. Chances are, you'll be able to tell right away what types of questions dominated. Or you could again talk to a student who has already had the class.

Why is it beneficial to know what kinds of questions to expect? Well, you'll probably need to know different types of information for different types of questions. **Objective** questions such as multiple-choice, true and false, matching, or fill-in-the-blank, for example, usually require you to know specific facts, such as names or dates. Essay questions, on the other hand, require you to be able to explain a concept in an organized manner. If you are studying the Boston Tea Party, for example, a multiple-choice question might require you to identify the

correct date of the event. An essay question, on the other hand, might ask you to explain the reasons for the Tea Party or summarize the results of the event.

The types of questions you expect to see on the test should also help to determine your study techniques. If you'll need to memorize facts, dates, or definitions, it can be a good idea to create flash cards. On one side of each card, write a question (or a word that needs to be defined). On the other side, write the answer. Then take the cards with you wherever you go. Whenever you have a spare moment, pull them out and go through them. As you get comfortable with the answers, make sure to mix the cards up so that you don't get so used to seeing the questions in a particular order that you can't answer them in any other order. As you memorize, you might also create mnemonic devices. Mnemonics are simply memory aids. For example, many people remember the

order of the colors in the rainbow with the mnemonic ROY G BIV. Each letter in the mnemonic stands for a color: red, orange, yellow, green, blue, indigo, violet. You can also create a silly sentence as a mnemonic. Each word in the sentence should begin with the letter of the items you are trying to remember. So, for the colors of the rainbow, you might think, "**R**achel, **o**nly **y**our **g**ood **b**rother **i**s **v**acuuming." Just make sure that your mnemonic isn't harder to remember than your material!

For an essay exam, an outline of possible questions and answers might help more than flash cards. Think about topics likely to appear as essay questions—often topics that can be explained, compared and contrasted, summarized, or argued. Then make an outline of the main points you would cover in such an essay, along with

supporting details. You could even go so far as to practice writing the essay. Even if the exact question doesn't appear on the test, at least you'll have gained practice in organizing your thoughts into a logical answer. If you are part of a study group, each group member can come up with a few practice essay questions. Then everyone can take turns answering some or all of the questions.

WRITE THE ANSWER

Practice tests work for other test types, too. If you have access to a previous year's test, you can use that as a practice test. And if not, you can make your own. Use homework questions or make up your own multiple-choice, true and false, or identification questions. Then give yourself a test (or trade

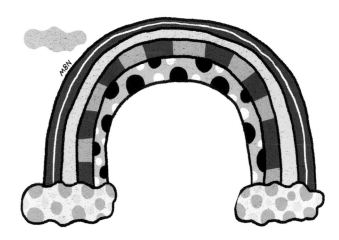

THE RIGHT ANSWER

with a friend) and see how you do.

By the time you have reviewed your notes and textbook, created flash cards, and outlined potential essay questions, you should feel as though you know the material backwards and forwards. And that's a good thing. You don't want to have to strain to come up with the right answer as you take the test—you want it to just be there. Be sure that you use your final study opportunity before the test to go over

any material that still eludes you. Remember that you may be nervous during the actual test, which could make it harder to recall information. But if you are over-prepared, you should be able to handle the pressure.

But what if, despite all of this good advice—and your best intentions—you find yourself completely unprepared the night before a test? Should you cram? As your last resort, yes. Just remember that no matter how hard

"UPON THE SUBJECT OF EDUCATION...I CAN ONLY SAY THAT I VIEW IT AS THE MOST IMPORTANT SUBJECT WHICH WE, AS A PEOPLE, CAN BE ENGAGED IN."

— Abraham Lincoln

you try, you are unlikely to be able to cram everything you need to know into your head in a few hours. So instead, pick out the five or six most important topics and study them intensely. Write them down—again and again. Recite them out loud—again and again. Make flash cards and review them—again and again. The key to cramming is repetition. You are trying to get the information to stick in your memory—at least until the test is done. By the time you've finished cramming, you'll likely be exhausted. So resolve to make this the last time you cram—and next time, study in advance!

CHAPTER
FOUR

TEST TIME

Well, it's the big day. And you're ready—you think. But you still have butterflies in your stomach. It's normal to be at least a little bit nervous before any big event, including an exam. But you don't want to be so nervous that it affects your ability to remember the information you've worked so hard to study. One of the best ways to deal with test anxiety is to be prepared—and you are, so remind yourself of that. In fact, you might even go so far as to **visualize** getting your test back with a bright red A marked on top. If you still feel nervous, try some relaxation techniques, such as deep breathing (breathe in slowly through your nose, then out through your mouth). Or, try tightening and relaxing your muscles one at a time to release extra tension. When you're done with that, ignore any anxiety that remains and get to the test. As you begin to answer the questions, your fear will likely fade into the background.

If you are anxious that you might forget important facts, consider jotting them in the **margin** as soon as you get your test paper. This way, you'll get them down while they're still fresh in your mind. You might write down special formulas, specific dates, or key names, for example.

Then, before you even begin to

mark any answers, glance through the whole test. This will give you an idea of how long the test is, what kinds of questions to expect, and how many points each section of the test is worth. Then you can plan your time accordingly. The test may be made up of 50 multiple-choice questions that count for half of your grade and an essay that counts for the other half, for example. So, you'll want to spend about half of your time on each section. If you spend so much time on the multiple-choice questions that you run out of time to write your essay, you'll lose half your grade. If you find that you're taking a long time on any one question, make a mark next to it. If you have time, you can come back to it later.

There is no rule that says you have to complete a test in order, either. Some people prefer to get the easier questions out of the way first so that they have more time to concentrate on the harder questions. Others like to do any essay questions first, then relax a bit as they tackle the objective questions. Use whatever technique works best for you. Just be sure that as you begin each section you pay careful attention to the directions.

In addition to these general test-taking strategies, you can make use of specific techniques to boost your score on different kinds of tests. Objective exams such as multiple-choice, true and false, and matching assess your ability to recognize the correct answer rather than your ability to explain or summarize a concept. Unlike **subjective** essay questions, which are graded based on your teacher's opinion of what you have written, objective questions have only one right answer—and either you know the answer or you don't.

The good news about multiple-choice questions is that you don't have to come up with the correct

"NOTHING CHEERS ME UP LIKE HAVING UNDERSTOOD SOMETHING DIFFICULT TO UNDERSTAND."

— G. C. Lichtenberg

ALWAYS EVERYONE NEVER

answer on your own. It's already on the page—you just have to recognize it. When dealing with multiple-choice, be sure to read the entire question (sometimes called the stem) first. Then try to come up with the answer before you even look at the answer choices. Once you have it, look through the answer options. If your answer is there, great! Mark it and move on. Be sure to read all the answer options thoroughly, though. Sometimes teachers can be tricky. They might throw in two similarly worded answer choices—but only one is correct. So make sure you've got the right one.

If you read the stem but can't come up with the answer in your head,

carefully read through all the answer choices. Cross out the ones you know are wrong. If you have only one option left, that's it. If you have more than one, consider which seems most correct. Watch for words such as "always," "never," or "everyone." These words often make an answer wrong (not many things are always or never true or apply to everyone). If you still can't eliminate an answer, guess. If you've narrowed your choice down to three answers, you have a 33 percent chance of guessing correctly.

True and false questions are similar to multiple-choice, except that instead of recognizing the correct answer, you need to recognize whether

READ ALL THE ANSWER OPTIONS THOROUGHLY

IF YOU STILL CAN'T ELIMINATE AN ANSWER, GUESS.

a specific statement is correct (true) or not (false). Remember that in order for a statement to be true, it must be true in its entirety. That means if even one word in it is incorrect, the whole statement is false. As with multiple-choice, be wary of statements that contain absolutes ("always," "everyone"). These are often false. Again, if you really don't know the answer, guess—you have a 50-50 chance of getting it right.

Matching questions also test your ability to recognize correct answers. Usually, matching tests consist of a list of questions in one column and a list of answers in another column. Before answering the questions, make sure you know whether each answer will be used only once or if some answers may be used multiple times. Then, as you begin with the first question, read through all of the answer choices. Make sure you choose the best one. If each answer will be used only once, cross off the answer choice you used—now you'll know

not to use it again. If you come to a question that you just can't find the answer to, skip it. When you're done with the rest of the answers, you may have only a few (or only one, if you're lucky) left—if so, that's the one you need.

Rather than testing your ability to recognize a correct answer, some objective questions test how well you can recall information. Fill-in-the-blank questions, for example, require you to come up with the missing word or phrase in a statement, without a list of answers to choose from. And identification questions often require that you define a word or describe a person or event in your own words. For these types of questions, thorough studying is your best ally. If you've memorized definitions and facts, you'll be able to handle these questions without a problem. Even if you only remember part of an answer, write it down—your teacher may give you at least some credit for it. For fill-in-the-blank questions, the

COMPARE AND CONTRAST

statement itself might give you a clue. The pronoun "she," for example, tells you that the answer is a woman, while the article "an" tells you that your answer needs to begin with a vowel (a, e, i, o, u).

Such hints won't help with essay questions, however. Here, you really have to know your stuff. Before beginning to answer an essay question, make sure you are absolutely positive of what the question asks. Do you need to explain a concept, compare and contrast two ideas, or summarize a story line? Underline key words in the question to help direct your thinking. Then take at least a few minutes to outline your answer to ensure that you will write an organized, cohesive essay. When it's time to write, start with the main idea—usually the question reworded as a **thesis statement**. From there, provide details and evidence to support the thesis.

If you run out of time to complete all of your essay questions, try to at least provide an outline for each one. This shows your teacher that you knew the answer to the question but didn't have time to finish it—and he may give you some credit for that. If you can't remember everything about a certain topic, write down what you do remember—again, you might get partial credit.

Once you've completed every part of the test, you may be tempted to turn it in as quickly as possible, especially if other students are doing so. Resist that temptation. If you have time left, return to the questions that stumped you earlier—the answers may come to you now, especially if another test question jogged your memory. Then review all your answers. If you think an answer is wrong, don't be afraid to change it. Also reread your essays. Make sure that you didn't miss any details. Now is a good time to correct any spelling or grammatical errors, too.

Then—and only then—turn in your test. Now you can relax. You've done it! Your dedication to studying your materials and learning test-taking techniques should earn you a grade that would make any teacher smile. And it should make you smile, too; after all, you've learned a new set of skills that you'll be able to make use of for the rest of your life!

Nature Sounds Awesome

GLOSSARY

accountable: responsible for something

adrenaline: a hormone released into the body in response to stress or fear, causing an increase in heart rate and blood pressure

auditory: having to do with the sense of hearing

civil service exam: a competitive exam required to attain certain government positions in law enforcement, the postal service, or administration

kinesthetic: having to do with body position and movement

margin: the white space at the sides of a printed piece of paper

motivated: determined or having a reason to do something

objective: having to do with facts and not influenced by opinions or feelings

role-playing: the acting out of a part

standardized tests: tests, often administered to a large number of students, on which the questions, test conditions, and scoring methods are the same for all test takers so that scores can be compared

subjective: based on opinions or feelings, rather than facts

thesis statement: a sentence that expresses the main ideas to be developed in an essay

visualize: to picture something in the mind

SELECTED BIBLIOGRAPHY

Coman, Marcia J., and Kathy L. Heavers. *Developing Study Skills, Taking Notes and Tests, Using Dictionaries and Libraries.* Lincolnwood, Ill.: NTC Publishing Group, 1998.

Ellis, Dave. *Becoming a Master Student.* 14th ed. Belmont, Calif.: Cengage Learning, 2011.

Fry, Ron. *How to Study.* 7th ed. Boston: Cengage Learning, 2012.

Hansen, Randall S., and Katharine Hansen. *The Complete Idiot's Guide to Study Skills.* New York: Alpha, 2008.

Kesselman-Turkel, Judi, and Franklynn Peterson. *Test-Taking Strategies.* Madison: University of Wisconsin Press, 2003.

Meyers, Judith N. *The Secrets of Taking Any Test.* 2nd ed. New York: LearningExpress, 2000.

Paul, Kevin. *Study Smarter, Not Harder.* 3rd ed. North Vancouver, B.C.: Self-Counsel Press, 2009.

The Princeton Review. *The Anxious Test-Taker's Guide to Cracking Any Test.* New York: Random House, 2009.

READ MORE

Bryfonski, Dedria, ed. *Standardized Testing*. Detroit: Greenhaven Press, 2012.

Fry, Ron. *"Ace" Any Test*. 6th ed. Boston: Course Technology, 2012.

Grossberg, Blythe N. *Test Success: Test-Taking and Study Strategies for All Students, Including Those with ADD and LD*. Plantation, Fla.: Specialty Press, 2009.

Johnson, Susan. *Taking the Anxiety Out of Taking Tests: A Step-by-Step Guide*. New York: Barnes & Noble Books, 2000.

WEBSITES

TeensHealth: Test Anxiety
http://kidshealth.org/teen/school_jobs/school/test_anxiety.html
Learn more about test anxiety—and how you can deal with it.

Test Taking Tips: Test-Taking Strategies, Skills, & Techniques
http://www.testtakingtips.com/test/index.htm
Get more tips for studying, taking tests, and dealing with test anxiety.

Virginia Standard of Learning Practice Tests
http://www.virginiasol.com/test.htm
Find practice tests in a variety of subject areas for all grade levels.

Note: Every effort has been made to ensure that the websites listed above are suitable for children, that they have educational value, and that they contain no inappropriate material. However, because of the nature of the Internet, it is impossible to guarantee that these sites will remain active indefinitely or that their contents will not be altered.

INDEX

anxieties 10, 13, 31, 35

cramming 11, 13, 31, 33

evaluations 7

learning 4–5, 7–8, 11, 13, 18, 22,
44
    types 18

memory 15, 28–29, 33, 44
    long-term 15, 33
    mnemonics 28–29

notes 11, 15–18, 22, 25, 29

questions 5, 13, 18, 26–29,
35–36, 38, 41, 43–44
    essay 13, 27–29, 36,
43–44
    fill-in-the-blank 27, 41
    matching 27, 36, 41
    multiple-choice 27, 29, 36,
38, 41
    objective 27, 36, 41
    subjective 36
    true and false 27, 36, 38

relaxation techniques 35–36,
44

reviewing 7, 15–18, 22, 25–26,
29, 31, 44

studying 4–5, 7–8, 10–11, 13,
15–18, 21–22, 25–29,
31, 33, 35, 41, 44
    in groups 18, 21, 29
    outlines 26–27, 29, 43
    plans 15–16, 22

test-taking skills 10, 13, 36,
44